Do-It-Yourself Retreat

The Spiritual Exercises of St Ignatius of Loyola

by
Fr André Ravier SJ

All booklets are published thanks to the
generous support of the members of the
Catholic Truth Society

CATHOLIC TRUTH SOCIETY
PUBLISHERS TO THE HOLY SEE

Contents

All rights reserved. This abridged version first published 2017 by The Incorporated Catholic Truth Society, 40-46 Harleyford Road London SE11 5AY Tel: 020 7640 0042 Fax: 020 7640 0046. © 2017 The Incorporated Catholic Truth Society. Original edition A Do-it-at-Home Retreat *© 1991 Ignatius Press. Reprinted with permission.*

ISBN 978 1 78469 157 8

Introduction

The *Spiritual Exercises* by St Ignatius of Loyola is quite obviously the book that has inspired this Do-It-Yourself Retreat. The plan we have carried out in this book in the pages that follow goes along with Ignatius' thinking. Did not he himself foresee that a person could make a retreat, in the true sense of the term, at home without ever interrupting his daily routine? And did not he indicate in his directives and annotations that the retreat should be adapted to the particular circumstances of the retreatant?

A retreat should be made in an atmosphere of complete spiritual freedom, under the inspiration of the Holy Spirit. This is why every retreat (irrespective of where it is made) is basically a personal experience.

We have kept intact the following points from St Ignatius' *Spiritual Exercises*:

- First of all, there is the primary purpose of the Exercises - namely, to turn from sin (or tepidity) to the good or the better.

- The necessary essentials, among which are, first and foremost, a fundamental "indifference" - that is, a freedom from everything that is not God, a resolute submission to his providential plan for me.

- The gradual unfolding of the order found in the Exercises: going from the Foundation and following through to the Contemplation To Attain and Live in the Love of God.

- The election - that is, the choice I make during the course of this spiritual experience to give order or an orientation to my life's direction.

- The principal themes and texts.

- The personal interchange between the retreatant and the spiritual director. This "touching base" with one another should take place at the very least occasionally - or, if it is necessary, it can take place by correspondence.

Despite their unique character, St Ignatius' Spiritual Exercises contain no particular spiritual doctrine. Rather, they present an art of teaching spiritual experience (either conversion or spiritual progress). They plot out the sure course, the dangers and illusions, the various conditions, the helps, and the impediments for attaining this end - all the while respecting God's complete liberty as well as the freedom of the soul of the person making the retreat. Essentially the Christian experience is the same for all, but it takes on a personal form for each individual. We have taken from this pedagogical method the explanations, advice and counsels (even those that are meant exclusively for the director) and have been faithful in recording them here.

The "retreat" we propose is an "immersion" (immersion connotes baptism) into the realities revealed to us by Jesus Christ through his Word, his death and his Resurrection. In fact, everything comes about between God, who beckons because he is love, and the human heart, which responds favourably to his invitation or rejects it. This acceptance or rejection takes place in that hidden and mysterious place St Francis de Sales calls "the heart of the heart".

Finally, we give this word of advice to the retreatant: when you are making your meditations or contemplations, always have your Bible or a copy of the New Testament at hand because Jesus Christ is the only source from which the soul, as well as the Church, can draw life.

Read the following points before beginning the retreat:

1. This retreat follows the *Spiritual Exercises*. What is the meaning of this term? It means every spiritual activity, such as the examination of conscience, meditation, contemplation, and vocal and mental prayer. Just as taking a walk, jogging, gymnastics and swimming are bodily exercises that get the body in shape and make it more alert, so we say that spiritual exercises are every method that firstly inclines the soul to purify itself, from anything that puts it in disorder and distances it from God, and then renders the soul more aware, more determined to seek and find what is the will of God in one's life: in this way the "interior man" is strengthened in faith, hope and love.

2. As a point of departure for almost every meditation a suitable biblical text is given. This text should be read as *lectio divina* - that is, with faith and feeling, by placing ourselves in the material place of the mystery that is being revealed to us. These texts are generally short, and the commentary on them is brief, intended merely to be suggestive. If the retreatant relies on the simple and basic presentation of facts in the mystery and then reflects on

it by himself, he may find through his own reasoning, illuminated by the Holy Spirit, something that enables him to penetrate deeper into the mystery. He will then gain more spiritual results and savour them better than if the director had explained to him the meaning of the text. It is not so much knowledge that fills and satisfies the soul but the intimate feeling and relish of what the mystery reveals.

3. This retreat is carried on over a period of eight days. It begins, however, with a fundamental meditation: God's call to man, whom he has created. This call is a call of love, and this fact should remain constantly present to the retreatant during the whole period of the retreat.

We do not mean to imply that each "day" is necessarily made up of twenty-four hours. Everything depends on the amount of time it takes the retreatant to attain the interior attitude sought in each particular session. This rhythm depends on the particular temperament of and grace given to each retreatant. For example, during the first part some may be more slow than others in coming to a repentance and sorrow for their sins. Therefore, it is necessary in each case to shorten or lengthen the session. The norm that determines this decision is whether or not the retreatant obtains the grace proper to the particular part, whatever the "state of his soul".

4. During the course of our meditation or contemplation, our interior attitude should be one of great reverence in regard to God our Lord, especially when we put into words whatever it is we are asking for, when we express our

sentiments or desires, and when we make some act of the will, such as a resolution, choice, or decision.

5. The attitude the retreatant must have - fundamental, indispensable, and unremitting - for making a good retreat is generosity towards our Creator and Lord. He should begin his retreat with an open heart and totally unsparing of self, offering to God his whole will and liberty, so that God may use who he is, and all that he has, according to his holy will.

6. It will be very helpful if the retreatant puts all of his effort into finding what he is looking for at the particular stage of the retreat he is at and does not busy himself considering meditations he will make in the future. Let him take each day as it comes, as if he had nothing to anticipate in the days that lie ahead. Let him be completely present to where he should be now and direct all his fervour to that topic alone.

7. The retreatant should give a full hour to each meditation or contemplation. This way he will be satisfied in knowing that he persevered in prayer during all of the allotted time. The reason for this is that, as a rule, our own apathy (and sometimes the devil) tempts us to cut short the time of prayer.

8. Take note: in times of fervour it takes little or no effort to spend a whole hour in contemplation, but in times of distress or boredom it is most painful to give the full time to prayer. Consequently, in order to put up a fight against this kind of desolation, the retreatant always ought to

remain in the Exercise a little more than the full hour. That way he will not only get used to resisting the temptation but he will also master it.

9. If by chance we have an inordinate attachment or inclination towards something or someone, it is very good to exercise all of our force in opposition to what we find is improperly so attractive. This way God can act with greater surety in our soul. For example, let us suppose someone is tempted to seek some kind of position, not for the honour and glory of God our Saviour nor for the spiritual welfare of his neighbour but for his own interest and personal advantage. This person should make an effort to bend his desires and efforts towards the opposite, and in his prayers he should beg God not to let him want that position or anything else unless the Divine Majesty orders his desires and regulates his first inclination to accept the position to correspond to God's will. As a result, the reasons that motivate him to take on something or to hold on to what he already has will be only the service, honour and glory of the Divine Majesty.

10. The retreatant will make his confession to a priest of his choice. Confession is one thing; the direction of the retreatant is something else. What is important is that the director help the retreatant. For this reason the retreatant, as far as he can, should be faithful in keeping the director informed about the different moods of his soul that come as a result of his temperament or from the action of the Holy Spirit or the devil. The advantage here is that during the

course of the retreat the director will be able to recommend some spiritual exercises best suited to the needs of the retreatant at the moment.

11. However little time the retreatant can give to the Exercises each day, it is essential that he create for himself a space where there is true solitude. If he cannot leave the house where he is living, he can at least withdraw to his room or to some other room apart from friends and from his daily occupations. This drawing himself apart has many advantages, but particularly these three:

First, as it costs him something, necessarily entailing some sacrifice, this separation from friends and occupations is of no little merit in God's eyes.

Second, because demands on the retreatant's attention coming from many quarters are reduced; he can then give his full attention to one single interest: the service of his Creator and his own spiritual progress. As a consequence, he will be more free to put to use all his faculties in seeking what he so wants to achieve.

Third, because experience proves that the more solitude and silence free the soul, the easier it is for it to approach God and wait for him. And the more our soul waits for him, the more likely it is that it will receive gifts from the Infinite Goodness of God.

12. The retreat supposes complete mutual confidence between the retreatant and the director. If the purpose of the one is not totally clear to the other, they should discuss the matter together with simplicity and charity.

Day

... ＇ *Was Created to Love God*

*That is, to praise, glorify and serve him and by
these means to achieve his eternal destiny.*
(This is the primary and fundamental aspect of my life.)

I exist...
What is the origin of this existence? Its meaning?
Its worth? This is the principal question that I should ask
myself as a human being.

The Bible, particularly the New Testament, answers it
for me in this way:

1. Man was created by God in his image and likeness.
Genesis 1:26-27: "God said, 'Let us make man in our own
image, in the likeness of ourselves.'"

"Because God is love" (*1 Jn 4:16*): man therefore is made
to love with his heart, which is like God's.

2. God created man to love him with all his heart, all his
mind and all his strength.

Deuteronomy 6:4-9: "'Hear, O Israel! The Lord is our
God, the Lord alone! Therefore, you shall love the Lord,
your God, with all your heart, with all your soul, with all
your strength. Take to heart these words that I enjoin on
you today. Drill them into your children. Speak of them
at home and abroad, whether you are busy or at rest. Bind

them at your wrist as a sign and let them be as a pendant on your forehead. Write them on the doorposts of your houses and on your gates.'"

Man loves God first of all through praise, adoration and service. It is along these lines that I should order - that is, regulate - all of my existence.

3. But love means more than this. Love of its very nature seeks union. God created man out of nothing to make him God's adoptive son in Jesus Christ and by Jesus Christ.

God's plan therefore consists in enabling us to participate here on earth (by faith and grace) and for all eternity (in a more intimate friendship) in the life of the Trinity.

"My dear people," John writes (*1 Jn* 3:2-3), "we are already the children of God, but what we are to be in the future has not yet been revealed; all we know is that when it is revealed we shall be like him because we shall see him as he really is."

At the Last Supper, after his farewell discourse and priestly prayer (*Jn* 13:31-17:26), it is Jesus himself who shows us the meaning of our existence in all of its magnificence. Let us relish words such as: "On that day you will understand that I am in my Father and you in me and I in you…. If anyone loves me he will keep my word, and my Father will love him and come to him and make our home with him" (*Jn* 14:19, 23). "I have given them the glory you gave to me, that they may be one as we are one. With me in them and you in me, may they be so completely one" (*Jn* 17:21).

We can deepen our appreciation of God's "hidden plan he so kindly made in Christ" for us by reading the first three chapters of St Paul's letter to the Ephesians: everything comes from God's love; everything should be returned to God in love.

4. I learn the answers to these questions through Jesus' response to the lawyer who asked him: "Master what must I do to inherit eternal life?" (*Lk* 10:25), or from the scribe who asked him, "Master, which is the greatest commandment of the law?" (*Mt* 23:34-40; *Mk* 12:28-34). He said, "You must love the Lord your God with all your heart, with all your soul, and with all your mind. This is the greatest and first commandment. The second resembles it: You must love your neighbour as yourself. On these two commandments hang the whole law, and the prophets also." And, according to Luke, Jesus said, "Do this and life is yours" (*Lk* 10:28).

At the end of these reflections it would be well to pray on the *Our Father, the Magnificat,* or simply on our *Act of Charity* according to the second or third method of prayer.

This fundamental truth regulates my relations with other men

And, in general, with all beings that enter into my life. It also governs my attitude with respect to all situations and events in which I find myself involved.

1. I do not exist alone on this earth. There are other creatures too - food, plants, animals. There are various conditions of body and soul: wealth and poverty, good health and bad, sadness and joy, success and failure, honours and humiliations. There are the circumstances of my state of life, my family life. And, most especially, there are other men who have the same divine destiny as myself.

It is necessary that I set up a network of ordered relationships with everything that is "created": ordered according to God's order, ordered according to the absolute, exclusive nature of his plan of love: "You worry about so many things, and yet few are needed, indeed only one" (*Lk* 10:42).

All created things wait for me to give them a meaning. For "the whole of creation is waiting with eagerness for the children of God to be revealed...with the intention that the whole creation itself might be freed from its slavery to corruption and brought into the same glorious freedom as the children of God" (*Rm* 8:19-21).

2. Here then is the rule that imposes itself on me: all things on the face of the earth are created for man to help him to achieve his destiny as a son of God.

From this it follows that man should make use of created things insofar as they help him in the attainment of his destiny and that he should have nothing to do with them insofar as they are an obstacle or hindrance to him.

In other words, I ought to love everything with the heart of a son - that is, according as God, my Father, wants each thing for me. And I ought to rid myself of them with the heart of a son, according as God, my Father, does not want them for me.

3. God manifests his will to me by his Providence as Creator (ordinarily he desires that man be healthy in mind and body, that families be united, that justice and love reign between men [see the Commandments, the counsels, the Beatitudes]). He does so through the teachings of his Son, Jesus Christ, and through what happens to me. His "order" is not a static, unchangeable order; it is a living order, revealing itself to me day in and day out, in the changing circumstances of my life; it is a dynamic order in which light and strength are together progressively revealed in my human conscience.

4. Because, at each instant, I conduct myself as a son of God with respect to every single "created thing", it is necessary that I remain indifferent to all created things as far as I am allowed free choice and as far as God does not prohibit me from choosing them. Consequently, for my part I do not will health more than sickness, riches more than poverty, honour more than dishonour, a long life rather than a short life, and so for all other things; but I will desire and choose

only those things that lead me to the end for which I was created - that is, to love God.

5. This fundamental indifference is a difficult yet critical way of looking at things. It must be understood in the light of the Gospel: to be indifferent means placing the love of God before every other love and every other aversion. It is living out charity.

Indifference is a free and deliberate choice: "I choose God…and with his grace, I shall always be faithful to this choice."

• Indifference, therefore, does not mean being unconcerned or insensitive: I can have a horror of sickness and death and yet love them because they are God's will for me, etc.

• Indifference does not take away those things I spontaneously find attractive or repulsive because of my personality or temperament, but I "accept" them only insofar as they concur with God's will for me. Indifference is a disposition of my freedom that makes no choice before knowing that God wants that which I choose.

• A "passion" ordered to God would be good; one that was inordinate or not disposed to his will would be evil. So it is a matter of "orienting" our temperament, our "heart" in a radical way. Compare the outbursts of anger and tenderness of St Paul: grace does not do away with these, but it directs them in terms of the love of Christ.

• Far from putting a damper on my enthusiasm for the projects of my personal, familial, professional or social life, indifference really stimulates them: it is God's will that "I am" and that I strive towards being, for myself, for others, and for the world more of what I am. At the same time, however, when the will of God is that I fail, that I become less important, or that I die, indifference enables me to accept failure, setback, death as a mysterious success: Did Christ save the world more by his work in Nazareth or his miracles and preaching than by his Passion?

• The type of the perfectly indifferent man is the one God called in the Bible "my just one" and "the man after my heart' - that is, Abraham, Job.

6. To sum up: indifference does not mean anything more than this profound, living disposition of spirit that enables me to choose this attitude freely with God's help: "God is everything for me; apart from him whatever is created is nothing. *Todo…nada.*"

My desire is to turn resolutely towards God and whatever God wants me to love.

Pray over these reflections:

• while slowly going over the *Act of Charity*;

• while making acts of offering - "I desire and choose God…I desire and choose whatever will draw me closer to God" - like the baptismal promises;

• while repeating: "Our Father…thy will be done on earth as it is in heaven".

Second Day
Looking at My Personal Sins

*Put yourself in the presence of God and make
the preparatory prayer. Ask him to inspire you.*

Composition of Place

I will ask for what I want and desire. Here it will be sincere
repentance and genuine sorrow for my sins.

First point: The review of my sins

I will call to mind all the sins of my life, reviewing my
life year by year or period by period. The following
classifications will help me in this consideration:

1. where I have lived;

2. my dealings with others;

3. what responsibilities I have had - my calling in life.

We should avoid, however, drawing up a juridical,
meticulous inventory, and even more we should watch out
for any type of scrupulosity. This review should be done
in the light of the Holy Spirit; that is to say, it should be
done in an atmosphere of adoration, gratitude and a deep
appreciation of a grace-filled life.

Second point: I will weigh my sins and the gravity of their disorder

Every capital sin - and to a certain extent any sin - is in itself a transgression against man's conscience and very often an offence against others. This is so even if God did not expressly forbid it. Sin, then, is a disorder in my own personal life and in my dealings with others.

Third point: I will honestly consider who I am before God

Who am I? (1) What am I compared to all men? (2) What are men compared with all the angels and saints? (3) What are all the angels and saints compared with God?

Then, considering just myself, what am I before God?

So it is this weak, finite being who stands up against God and says, "I will not serve. I will not obey." There is something in common with Satan's revolt at the core of every sin.

Being aware of what my sins are in reality - even those that at the time seemed to me to be of little consequence, but to which I fully consented - makes me conclude that I have preferred myself to God.

Fourth point: I will turn towards God and say to him…

Who are you, Lord? Who are you?

And I will in this way compare his wisdom with my ignorance, his power with my weakness, his justice with my iniquity, his goodness with my wickedness, his love with my selfishness, etc. The gravity of sin and the pains of hell are understood properly only when we contrast them with "the extraordinary love with which God has loved us".

Fifth point: Profound wonder but also immense gratitude now overwhelm me

The Lord spared me at the time of my sin. Creation did not rise up against me but remained subdued, supportive, while I was saying "no" to the Creator. God's work of creation continued on for me and for my enjoyment. Had I really been aware of this patience of his, "a cry", in St Ignatius' words, "of wonder accompanied by surging emotion" would have escaped my lips. And then there is St Bruno's aspiration: "Oh, pure goodness!"

I will conclude my meditation by addressing a prayer first to our Lady. I will ask her to obtain for me three graces from her Son: (1) the grace to see my sin with his eyes and to detest it as he detests it; (2) the grace to feel, even to the point of experiencing shame, an abhorrence for the disorder of what is sinful in my life so that I can put it in order; (3) the grace to discern what is good and what is evil in the world so that detesting what is evil I can put it away from me. I will then say a *Hail Mary*.

Afterwards I will make the same petitions to Jesus, asking that he obtain from his Father these graces for me. Then I will say some prayer such as the *Body of Christ*.

Finally, I will address the Father, asking that he, the Lord eternal, grant me these three graces. Then I will say an *Our Father*.

Colloquy of Mercy

Repetition is a most effective exercise. We shall use it here.

*Put yourself in the presence of God and make
the preparatory prayer. Ask him to inspire you.*

Composition of Place

"Imagine Christ our Lord present before you nailed to the Cross…seeing him in this plight, nailed to the Cross."

Let us look closely at our crucifix: we stand before him with the burden of our personal sins and also, because we are members of the Church, with the weight of the sins of the world.

I will ask for what I want and desire:

• in the light of the Cross of Christ better to understand interiorly the mystery of sin;

• to see and understand sin as God sees and understands it, not as the world judges it.

First point: "Asking him how it is that though he is the Creator, he has become man"

Indeed, this is a mystery. To appreciate it, we must ask God himself. He alone can respond.

Let us slowly read the passage where St Paul expresses his astonishment and admiration in Philippians 2:6-7: Jesus Christ, "being in the form of God, did not count equality with God something to be grasped at. But he emptied himself, taking the form of a slave, becoming as human beings are."

This is the first step of the Son of God's self-abasement.

Indeed, the Word of God's way of proceeding is exactly the opposite of the way a sinner operates.

• Revolt is the motivation for the sinner. For Christ it is selflessness and obedience.

• For the sinner it is pride. For Christ it is stripping himself of his divine prerogatives; it is humility and even embracing humiliations.

With him how far we are from any type of love that is conditional, calculated!

Verbum caro…The Word was made flesh…Adore… What a refinement of human nature!

"You will be like gods", Satan said to the man and woman, and they sinned.

And now that has been realised, and even more than realised: man, in uniting himself with the Word Made Flesh, becomes a son of God, is "one" with God.

Second point: "How is it that he has passed from eternal life to death here in time?"

This is the second cause of astonishment, the mystery that is even more bewildering than the Incarnation: he who is presented to us as Life everlasting ("I am the Life", "I am the Resurrection and the Life") knows death in time, death on the Cross.

In the passage from Philippians cited above, St Paul describes Christ's death on the Cross as the final step in all his actions of self-abasement: "And being in every way like a human being, he was humbler yet, even being obedient unto death, death on a cross" (*Ph* 2:7-8).

Indeed, this death of God on a cross is a stumbling block and folly for men. As St Paul wrote: "We are preaching a crucified Christ: to the Jews an obstacle they cannot get over, to the gentiles foolishness, but to those who have been called…a Christ who is both the power of God and the wisdom of God" (*1 Co* 1:23).

Before, death had been an obstacle and a scandal to human intelligence, but how much more of an obstacle and scandal is it when it includes him who said that he was "Life Everlasting"? Only the Resurrection could solve - up to a point - this problem and resolve this apparent contradiction.

And yet Jesus Christ went even as far as that.

Third point: The only response to these two "How is it that?"

Only one answer: "God is love" (*1 Jn* 4:8).

"God so loved the world that he sent his only son" (*Jn* 3:16).

"Love consists in this: it is not we who loved God, but God loved us and sent his Son to expiate our sins" (*1 Jn* 4:10).

But if so much love was necessary to make amends for our sins, then sin is a grave matter, infinitely grave. Is it not true that on the moral and spiritual plane it is the most grave matter there is?

Indeed. For it ruins "the purpose and good pleasure" that God had determined for man from all eternity. It would take the Passion and death of God to reintroduce us into the intimacy of the Trinity.

Fourth point: "Then I will reflect upon myself and ask: 'What have I done for Christ? What am I doing for Christ? What ought I to do for Christ?'"

I will look at myself now as I am at the present moment. What is the connection between me now and what I have been meditating on? I should see my life only in the light of the love with which I am loved. The law of love is exacting. St Ignatius remarked: "It is good to call attention to two points: the first is that love ought to manifest itself in deeds rather than in words." The second is that "love consists in a mutual sharing of goods".

1. "What have I done for Christ?" More of a confusion and shame about myself and about the niggardliness and lukewarmness of my love than about my sins, which I should not bother to enumerate.

2. "What am I doing for Christ?" The mediocrity of my life. My defects. My lack of purpose and courage.

3. "What ought I to do for Christ?" A firm purpose. An ideal in life that goes beyond the firm purpose. St Paul's message to the Colossians maps out for us the way to love: "I make up for what is lacking in the sufferings of Christ for the sake of his body, the Church" (*Col* 1:24).

Let us note "for Christ", a phrase that is repeated over and over again like a refrain. We are not face to face with a code, a law, but with Someone who loves us and who calls us to love in return: "Everything in Christianity", Claudel said, "always comes down to a face-to-face encounter."

———

I will end this meditation (which is merely a long dialogue with Christ) with a most intimate *Our Father*, which I will recite very slowly. God's plan for man and for creation is contained in its entirety in this prayer, "which our Saviour has taught us".

Third Day
The Call of Christ, Our Leader

*Contemplated through the symbolic call
of an earthly king.*

1. This juncture in the Exercises poses a very serious problem for us: Who should go beyond this point to continue the retreat? In the Eighteenth Annotation St Ignatius writes:

> If the director sees that the retreatant has little aptitude or little natural ability, that he is one from whom little fruit is expected…let him go no further to take up matters of election on the choice of the way of life and any other Exercises that are outside the First Week.

This ability to proceed further is a gift, but it should be understood as the ability of a person to live the spiritual life in the fervour and generosity of love. Never did St Ignatius exclude from the Christian elite the humble, the uneducated or the poor of spirit. His experience was like that of St Francis de Sales, who confessed: "I have found God full of sweetness and perfume among the highest and hardiest mountains, where many simple souls cherish him and adore him in complete truth and sincerity." So we should read in St Ignatius' wise recommendation nothing more than that every retreat should be adapted to the temperament and the grace of the retreatant.

2. In Christian life there are not two faiths, two hopes and two charities (see *Ep* 4:5). All the baptised have the vocation to be "perfect as [their] heavenly Father is perfect" (*Mt* 5:48). But there are hundreds of degrees of generosity, hundreds of ways to distinguish oneself in his service, and these differences depend on temperament and grace.

3. The image of the temporal king - an image borrowed from the chivalry of Ignatius' time - may cause problems for some people today. If such is the case, they should recall the image some of the Jews had about the Messiah at the time of Christ - that is, that he should be a military leader, God's Chosen One who would restore the kingdom of Israel and lead her people to victory and to the conquest of the world. If the Biblical image of a military leader shocks some, then these people might substitute for it a political figure, or an inspired thinker, a great reformer, or an academic leader.

Place yourself in the presence of God and make the prayer beginning the meditation considering how God watches you. Then make the act of reverence and humility. Ask him to inspire you and help you.

Composition of Place

This will be to see with the imagination the synagogues, villages and towns where Christ our Lord preached.

I will ask for what I want and desire. Here it will be for the grace not to be deaf to the Lord's call but to be prompt and diligent to accomplish his most holy will.

In the first part, let us contemplate the call of an outstanding king, chosen by God

First point: Earthly king

I will imagine an earthly king chosen by God our Lord himself, to whom all Christian princes and people pay respect and obedience. He is therefore a leader who enjoys the prestige of having been the one chosen out of all Christendom by God himself, an extraordinary chief whose programme and whose promises are wonderful.

Second point: This king speaks

I will consider how this king speaks to all his own: "My will is to conquer all the lands of the infidels. Therefore, whoever would wish to come with me must be content with the same food as I, the same drink, the same clothing, etc. He must also labour with me by day and watch with me by night, etc., so that he can share with me in victory just as he has shared with me in suffering."

The conditions for being a companion of the king are therefore most exacting and demanding. Accepting companionship with him implies a "co-sharing" with him in the strictest sense of the term - that is, it covers all of the circumstances and every moment of one's whole life. It means partaking of his toil and sufferings as well as of his victory, which from this moment on has been guaranteed.

Third point: Answer to this king

I will consider what type of an answer his faithful subjects will give a king who is so generous and so compelling. If anyone refused the invitation from such a king, he would deserve to be reprimanded and considered fainthearted.

Here we are introduced to an extremely important feature in the spiritual teaching of St Ignatius, his appeal to the "heart" of a person, to his noble-mindedness, his affinity for deep, intimate friendship, generosity, enthusiasm. We are reminded here of the advice we gave the retreatant before beginning the Exercises, namely that his primary disposition for receiving gifts and favours from God should be generosity, offering his entire will and liberty to God so that he may dispose of him, make use of him, according to his will.

The second part of the Exercise consists in applying the example of this king to Christ our Lord

First point: Facts and reality

The whole scope of this contemplation is in St Ignatius' question "How much more…?", and then his invitation to the retreatant to draw the inferred conclusion.

If an invitation of an earthly king to his subjects is so wonderful, how much more is it worthy of consideration that we look at Christ our Lord, the eternal King, who invites the whole universe and at the same time each person in particular to come before him. To these he says, "It is my will to conquer the whole universe and all my enemies and thus to enter into the glory of my Father. Therefore, whoever wishes to come with me should labour with me, so that in following me in suffering he may follow me also in glory."

We are in a setting that is right out of the Gospels:

1. Jesus is the eternal King.

2. His call is made to the heart of each person. "Follow me." "If anyone wants to be a follower of mine, let him renounce himself and take up his cross and follow me" (*Mt* 16:24; *Mk* 8:34). "No one who does not carry his cross and come after me can be my disciple" (*Lk* 14:27).

3. His purpose is to "recapitulate" in himself the whole universe, visible and invisible. In the text of the Ephesians upon which we have already meditated, St Paul writes: "[God the Father] has let us know the mystery of his purpose, the hidden plan he so kindly made in Christ from the beginning to act upon when the times had run their course to the end: that he would bring everything together under Christ as head, everything in the heavens and everything on earth" (*Ep* 1:9-10).

4. Moreover, the victory in Christ's battle is already certain: "I have conquered the world", he says at the hour of his Passion (see *Jn* 16:33).

Second point: The first response

I will consider that all those who have sound judgment will offer themselves unreservedly for this task.

Very important: the invitation is the same to all; the difference comes in the responses. Christ our Lord invites all men: "Be perfect, as your heavenly Father is perfect" (*Mt* 5:48). Each one responds to this call according to his grace, in the mystery of his personal fidelity.

This first response is already very lofty. It is total, without reserve. Everything is accepted. But between this response and that of the insignes - that is, those who "distinguish or signalise" themselves - there is a distance that separates the love that comes from making a choice from reasonable motivations, including even personal interests, and a pure, unselfish love that is willing to take risks in the unconditional gift of self.

Third point: The response of the insignes

These make the same response as those who are reasonable, but they make it differently. They make it with their whole heart.

Those who shall be more desirous to show affection and signalise themselves in entire service of their King and Lord of all will not only offer themselves entirely for the work but, more, will also act against their selfishness and against all worldly love and make offerings of greater value and more importance, saying:

> Eternal Lord of all things, I make my offering with your favour and help, before your Infinite Goodness and before your glorious Mother and all the saints of your heavenly court; I want and desire, and this is my deliberate choice, provided that it is only for your greater service and praise, to imitate you in bearing all injustices and contempt, and all poverty, both real and spiritual, if your Most Holy Majesty wishes to choose and admit me into this state of life.

We should carefully note that in this offering there is no question of religious life, or of religious poverty, but of the evangelical poverty of the Christian.

It is possible that we would falter before making such an offering. Some might then advise us to ask God at least for the desire to desire to make such an offering. But it would be better to say: consider to what extent Christ has loved you. "[He] loved me and gave himself for me" (*Gal 2:20*). And then, relying on his grace, agree to go wherever he would like you to go. Say with St Paul: "*Scio cui credidi*" (I know in whom I have put my trust) (*2 Tm 1:12*).

Important note: It is obvious that this contemplation is connected with everything Jesus Christ has revealed to us about the "Kingdom of God" and the "Kingdom of heaven" and, as a consequence, with everything that touches on preaching the Gospel in the world and with the mission of the Church here on earth. This is a meditation that is far-reaching and very difficult because the distinction between "temporal" and "spiritual" is complex, yet this distinction is of paramount importance. Reread, for example, the bewildering dialogue between Jesus and Pilate: "'So, then you are a king?' Jesus answered, 'It is you who say that I am a king. I was born for this; I came into the world for this: to bear witness to the truth" (*Jn 18:37*; cf. *19:13-16, 19-23*). Then recall that the apostles found it difficult indeed to free themselves from the image of a military Messiah in charge of a temporal kingdom (*Ac 1:6-9*). Then there is the example of Paul, who had no hesitation about taking his images out of a military armoury: "Put on the full armour of God… And then you must take salvation as your helmet and the sword of the Spirit, that is, the Word of God" (*Ep* 6:10-17).

Beginning with the current Exercise and during the rest of the retreat it will be most profitable to spend some time reading the Bible (especially the New Testament) or some life of a saint. The important thing is to choose these readings to complement the spirit of the meditations of the particular part of the Exercises where one finds oneself.

The "with me" in Christ's call as seen from St Paul's perspective

What are the elements that go into making up the mystical life of a Christian? St Paul gives the complete answer to this question when he writes to the Galatians (2:20): "I have been crucified with Christ, and yet I am alive; yet it is no longer I, but Christ living in me."

The mystical life is essentially "being united" with Jesus Christ and through him with the Father. It consists of growth in grace, and grace is simply God's life, the divine life in us. The mystical life of a Christian is therefore a growth in faith, hope and charity. Here on earth the culmination of this life is the martyr, the one who dies with Jesus Christ to live with Jesus Christ.

Consequently this life consists of entering into the mystery of Jesus in order to die with him so that I can be raised up with him. This is the life of the "new creature" that here on earth we live through faith and hope and that after our death we shall live in the full light of the vision of glory.

In order to express this reality of our Christian life, of living out this unity with Christ in life and in death, St Paul has created a whole vocabulary of verbs that begin with the prefix *sun* in Greek (*cum* in Latin), that is, "with". A meditation on the call of the King from St Paul's point of view will enable us to see his call and also his Kingdom in their various spiritual dimensions.

Place yourself in the presence of God and say the prayer to begin the meditation. Ask him to inspire you.

Composition of Place

Either Jesus speaking with Nicodemus on the need for man's being "reborn" (*Jn* 3:3-4) or on Calvary at the time when the centurion's lance pierces Jesus' side (*Jn* 19:34).

I will ask for what I want and desire. Here, I will ask not to be deaf to the call of the eternal King but to be prompt and diligent to accomplish his most holy will.

First point: Baptism: "Plunged" into Jesus' death in order to be raised up with Jesus

It is baptism (and the act of faith that it supposes) that transforms us with Jesus Christ into sons of God.

Romans 6:2-11: "Are you not aware that we who were baptised into Christ Jesus were baptised into his death? Through baptism into his death we were buried with him so that, just as Christ was raised from the dead by the glory of the Father, we too might live a new life." In verse 5 St Paul insists: "If we have been united with Christ [*complantati*] through likeness to his death, so shall we be through a like resurrection."

What is the life of Christ? After our baptism, what is our life? "His life is a life for God. In the same way, you must consider yourselves dead to sin but alive for God in Christ Jesus."

Second point: *In novitate vitae* ("in a new life")

The effect of baptism is immediate. Our spiritual resurrection is not the same as the resurrection to come. It is a resurrection in faith, one that has taken place here and now.

As of now we are the "resurrected". What does this mean?

1. It means we are "dead to sin" and that as a result we must, with Christ, fight against all of his "enemies" - that is, against our concupiscence and selfishness: "Our old self was crucified with Christ to the Cross" (*Rm* 6:6). "God has rescued us from the power of darkness and brought us into the kingdom of his beloved Son. Through him we have redemption, the forgiveness of our sins" (*Col* 1:13-14).

"All of you who have been baptised into Christ have clothed yourselves with him" (*Gal* 3:27).

The result of this is that we go beyond "co-sharing with Christ" in his work to a veritable unity in Christ. In order to express this marvellous and mysterious reality, St Paul created a formula that has no equivalent anywhere in the Greek language: *en Christo*, that is, "in Christ".

2. What we have become, in Jesus Christ the Son of God, and what we will be in the future are explained to us by St Paul in his Epistle to the Romans (8:16-17): "You have

received a spirit of adoption through which we cry out, 'Abba' [Father]. The Spirit himself gives witness with our spirit that we are children of God. But if we are children, we are heirs as well: heirs of God, heirs with Christ, if only we suffer with him so as to be glorified with him." The Holy Spirit is the great craftsman in creating our unity with Christ, and he does so just as he unites the Father and the Word in the Trinity.

3. The three theological virtues accompany divine grace in us:

Faith, which enables us to live the invisible and makes the invisible present, real, to us.

Hope, which enables us to possess the invisible now.

Charity, which unites us with the invisible.

These virtues reach their fullness according to how the Christian lives out his baptismal grace and how he progresses in becoming united with Christ. They always remain the "rock" upon which his total Christian life is built.

Third point: Progress in unity with Christ

As long as we are on this earth, this "new life", which we receive in baptism and in our initial act of faith, should expand and grow.

1. This growth always takes place with Christ, in terms of the regular pattern of death and resurrection, as it appears:

a. through the sacramental life, particularly in the Eucharist.

b. by our acceptance of our human condition, that is, our death and everything that prefigures that death in us.

It is the deepening of St Paul's statement: "In my own flesh I fill up what is lacking in the sufferings of Christ for the sake of his body, the Church" (*Col* 1:14).

c. through all that we do on both the purely human and the spiritual levels. It is through our activities that we are engaged here on earth in the very same combat in which Christ was involved.

d. through our life of serious prayer. By our contemplation and through the mediation of love, our prayer becomes divine life within us: "The Spirit too helps us in our weakness, for we do not know how to pray as we ought; but the Spirit himself makes intercession for us with groanings that cannot be expressed in speech" (*Rm* 8:26).

2. Through an intensification and a purification of faith, hope, and charity within us. We can come to appreciate the usefulness of "nights", whatever their origin-from the spirit or the senses because they strip away from us everything that is nonessential, and they force us to centre ourselves on God alone.

3. Everything in our lives that appears to us, either from close range or from afar, to be associated with the witness of the martyr (trials, persecutions, religious vows) is of the greatest worth in uniting us with Christ, in "plunging" us into the mystery of his death and Resurrection.

Fourth point: It is in heaven where the full maturation of this grace is realised. There we, who have suffered with Jesus Christ, will be victorious with him

1. There is only a flimsy veil between grace and glory. If, as St John says, "we are God's children now, what we shall be later has not come to light…when it comes to light we shall be like him, for we shall see him as he is" (*1 Jn* 3:2); then, between grace and glory there is only "a twinkling of an eye [*ictus oculi*]" (*1 Co* 15:52).

2. Yet, from now on, this "new life" must be seen as reality, and our eyes must see all things as God sees them: "New heavens and a new earth" (*Rv* 21), because for the person who lives in faith, hope, and charity, heaven is already here on earth.

———

I will carry on a conversation with Jesus Christ in which I will renew my offering of service in the Kingdom to him. And I will listen to him say to me: "*Dilexi te*…I love you, and I have delivered myself for you."

I will also talk over all of this with the Blessed Virgin Mary, asking her that I may "be placed with Jesus Christ" (St Ignatius summed up in this formula his whole notion of sanctity), and I will ask her to teach me to be content to be "the companion of Jesus", to be "one" with him. "This alone is enough for me", as the dying St Bernadette said, clasping her crucifix.

I will conclude with the *Our Father* and the *Hail Mary*.

Fourth Day
The Mystery of the Incarnation

*Place yourself in the presence of God and make
the preparatory prayer. Ask him to help you.*

I will call to mind the history of the subject that I will contemplate. Here it will be from St Paul's Epistle to the Galatians (4:3-6): "In the same way, while we were not yet of age we were like slaves subordinated to the elements of the world; but when the designated time had come, God sent forth his Son born of a woman, born under the law, to deliver from the law those who were subjected to it, so that we might receive our status as adopted sons." This contemplation will then unfold like a triptych with three panels side by side. In the first panel we see the three Divine Persons, how they are looking down on the whole expanse of the world filled with men who live under the slavery of sin. In the central panel we see them determining from their eternity to send the Second Person to become man to save the human race. Finally, in the third panel we see that when the fullness of time arrives, they send the Angel Gabriel to our Lady. At each point of my contemplation I will return to these three scenes of the triptych.

Let us now follow up on the realities that these Biblical scenes represent and on the particular historic event that is taking place.

Composition of Place

Here I will see the great extent of the earth's surface, where so many people of so many diverse backgrounds have lived in the past, are living in the present, and will live in the future.

Especially I will consider the house and room of our Lady at Nazareth in Galilee, seeing it as a place of light amid so much darkness and shadows.

I will ask for what I want and desire. Here it will be an interior knowledge of the Lord, who is made man for me so that I may love him more and follow him more closely.

First point: I will look at the persons depicted in these scenes

1. The various people throughout the world. I will see them in their great variety of dress and ways of living, where they are, and what kind of civilisations they have: some are white, others black; some are at peace, others at war; some are weeping, others laughing; some are in good health, others sick; some are being born, others dying.

We have here the same theme of contrasts and the same kind of description as we find in Ecclesiastes 3:2-9: "A time to be born and a time to die". All of this is quite existential. The stress is on a real awareness of the human condition in its diversity and its contrasts.

This pagan world is a world of slavery, rivalries, war, hate. Except for a few people of goodwill, or the "just" who have remained upright, it is a world that never witnesses an act of the love of God or hears a cry of fraternal charity.

2. I will see and consider the three Divine Persons, enthroned in their majesty. They look upon the whole world and all the people who are living in such blindness and corruption. What has become of the people whom they created "in their own image and likeness"? In what a state do they live and die!

3. I will look at Mary at prayer in her room in Nazareth, and I will consider the angel greeting her. Full of grace, full of love for God, full of love for men.

I will reflect on these scenes and draw spiritual profit from them.

Second point: I shall listen to the words spoken

1. What are the people saying? What does their speech mean as they converse with one another? How many lies, examples of false witness, errors, etc.? How often do they speak to God or against God? Let us reflect for a moment on the "news" diffused today throughout the world by the press and all types of mass media.

2. What are the three Divine Persons saying? Eternal words! Just as one day they said, "Let us make man in our own image, after our likeness" (*Gn* 1:26), today they say, "Let us redeem the human race."

And I will reflect on what St John said: "Yes, God so loved the world that he gave his only Son" (*Jn* 3:16). "God's love was revealed in our midst in this way: he sent his only Son to the world that we might have life through him" (*1 Jn* 4:9).

I will also reflect on what St Paul wrote to the Ephesians (1:4): "God chose us in him [our Lord Jesus Christ] before the world began, to be holy and blameless in his sight, to be full of love…through Christ Jesus to be his adopted sons." The unique and eternal Word of God!

3. Reread the Gospel account of the remarkable conversation between the Virgin Mary and the Angel Gabriel at the Annunciation (*Lk* 1:26-38).

I will reflect on all I hear to draw spiritual profit from these words.

Third point: I will look closely at the actions
of the persons depicted in these scenes

Actions reveal what is in the heart; they disclose our deepest feelings, and they measure the amount of our love.

1. The men on the face of the earth. How far are we from the new commandment: "Love one another!" The world is an extended battlefield where each person looks out for his own interests, every one of which is determined by his ambition, passions, and covetous desires.

2. The Father who "sends" his Son. His Son replies, "I am here, Father, to do your will!" The Father pardons men; the Son offers himself and delivers himself to them. The divine "mission" is thereby begun - a mission that, after the death, Resurrection and ascension of Jesus, will be carried out by the Holy Spirit until the end of the world.

3. The *Verbum caro factum est* (the Word was made flesh) is fulfilled in Mary. Let us adore in silence.

Let us give the full sense, the real, and the very concrete sense to this "*caro factum est*" as St Paul does: "His Son, who was descended from David according to the flesh" (*Rm* 1:3); "from them [our fathers] came the Messiah (I speak of his human origins)" (*Rm* 9:5).

This realism is very important for the accuracy of our religious thinking on this subject of the Incarnation. We must eliminate from such terms as the Eucharist, the Cross, the Resurrection, and the Divine Motherhood anything that smacks of the hazy or the fuzzy. We are dealing here with reality, a reality even more real than that grasped by our senses.

Even in his time, St John bewailed the false teachings regarding the Incarnation: "Many deceitful men have gone out into the world, men who do not acknowledge Jesus Christ as coming in the flesh" (*2 Jn* 7).

I will look at our Lady as she humbles herself and gives thanks to the Divine Majesty.

I will then draw spiritual profit from the considerations on this point.

Finally, I will converse with the three Divine Persons, with the eternal Word incarnate and with the Virgin Mary, asking them, according to inspirations I now feel within me, to help me in every way to follow more closely and imitate better our Lord, who has just now become man "for me": "He loved me, and he became incarnate for me."

I will end my contemplation with an *Our Father* and, with the angel at the Annunciation, I shall repeat the *Hail Mary*.

Fifth Day
A Meditation on Two Standards

*The one of Christ, our Supreme Leader and Lord,
the other of Lucifer, the Enemy of God and Man.*

*Place yourself in the presence of God and make
your preparatory prayer. Ask him to inspire you.*

I will call to mind the history

Using Ignatian imagery, I will consider the profound drama
of humanity. This consists, as St John expresses it, in the
struggle between Darkness and Light, or, in the thinking
of St Paul, in the struggle between Spirit and Flesh, or, as St
Augustine visualises it, in the struggle between the City of
God and the City of Man. On the one hand I will picture
Christ, who calls and who wishes to unite all men, and on
the other I will imagine Lucifer, who draws men away from
Christ and makes them his own disciples.

Composition of Place

If it helps me, I will see in my imagination two plains. One
is a great plain around Jerusalem, where our Lord, the
sovereign Leader of the "just", stands. The other plain is
around the region of Babylon, and here is where Lucifer,
the enemy of Christ and the enemy of our human nature,
takes his place.

If this tableau seems to me to be too imaginative, I will picture Christ our Lord before me. It is evening, and he appears tired after a whole day of preaching. He is engaged in an evaluation of his apostolate, balancing hostility or indifference (which he meets uninterruptedly and with every step he takes) with the love that he awakens in a number of hearts, the joy he communicates, and the glory that he gives to his Father.

I will ask for what I want and desire. Here I will ask for a knowledge of the tactics of Lucifer and for help and grace to guard myself against them. I will also ask for a knowledge of the true life, which our true and sovereign Leader, Jesus Christ, teaches, and for the grace to imitate him.

First Part

First point: I will imagine Lucifer in his camp

If it helps, the retreatant should read the description of Lucifer in the twelfth chapter of the book of Revelation: "The huge dragon, the ancient serpent known as the devil or Satan, the seducer of the whole world." Or one can more simply, and with more realism, picture what the Gospel pejoratively calls "the world", using as an example some of our modern "Babylons": where Lucifer is with all his seductions, all his snares, all his tactics for lying and for blinding and even corrupting every man's conscience.

Second point: I will consider Lucifer's activity

He makes his presence universal, either directly or through his demons, or through perverse men - sending some to this city or that, throughout the whole world, so that no province, no place, no state of life, no single person is overlooked.

Consider the text: "Enraged at her [the Virgin Mary's] escape, the dragon went off to make war on the rest of her offspring, on those who keep God's commandments and give witness to Jesus."

Third point: Lucifer's tactics

Consider the discourse Lucifer addresses to those he scatters throughout the world. In essence it comes down to this: they are first of all to tempt men through their cravings for riches (this is the way it usually all begins) so that men will then more readily be carried away by the empty honours of this world and finally by overweening pride. Therefore, the first step is wealth and the power it brings; the second, worldly honour and the third, pride. By these three passions, the devil will lead a man to all the other vices.

We recognise in this description the three "concupiscences" about which St John writes (*1 Jn* 2:15-16): "If anyone loves the world, the Father's love has no place in him, because everything that there is in the world - disordered bodily desires, disordered desires of the eyes, pride in possession - is not from the Father, but it is from the world."

Second Part

We should now imagine Christ our Lord, our sovereign and true Chief, in a way that is the total opposite of Lucifer's.

First point: I will consider Christ our Lord

In the plain around Jerusalem where he so often travelled during his earthly life. His attitude is humble; his appearance handsome, attractive, noble-minded. Grace radiates from his whole person. He is one of those men who attract and fascinate others solely by the force of his presence; his enemies regarded him as a seducer.

Second point: I will consider the words that Christ our Lord addresses to all his servants and friends

As he sends them throughout the world, he commissions them to search out all men of any and every condition and to help them:

1. first of all, by attracting them to seek the highest spiritual poverty and, should the Divine Majesty be better served and will it, even to embrace actual poverty;

2. and then by leading them to the desire to strive for (or at least to esteem) humiliations and contempt. For it is from humiliations and contempt that a person is led to humility - that is, to a sense of reality about our human condition.

So there will be three steps in our approach to evangelical perfection:

• The first is poverty as opposed to riches.

• The second is humiliations and contempt as opposed to worldly honour.

• The third is humility as opposed to pride.

By these three steps, Christ's servants and friends lead men to all the other virtues.

I will talk this matter over with our Lady, asking her that she obtain for me from her Son and Lord the grace to be received under his standard:

1. in the highest spiritual poverty and, should the Divine Majesty be better served and pleased to choose me, even in actual poverty;

2. so as to imitate him more, in accepting all the humiliations and injustices that come into my life, provided that I can take on these without causing anyone to sin and without offence to the Divine Majesty.

I will recite a *Hail Mary*.

I will make the same prayer to her Son, asking him to obtain for me the same graces from his Father. And I will say the prayer *Soul of Christ*.

I will ask the Father to grant me these same graces. And I shall say an *Our Father*.

Three classes of men - faced with making what seems to them to be the best decision.

This Exercise is made within the context of the Meditation on Two Standards. Its purpose is to help us decide on the option that seems to us to conform best to the will of God for us. St Ignatius chose poverty or the sincere desire to give up a certain amount of money as a theme that has inspired this Exercise. A person can also substitute honours, success, a social position - anything that stands for wealth and power in the eyes of men.

Place yourself in the presence of God and make the prayer to begin the Exercise. Ask him to inspire you.

I will place before my mind's eye the history St Ignatius proposes. There are three classes of men. Each one of them has acquired a certain sum of money, but it is not solely from the love of God that they have become rich. All three groups wish "to save their souls" and find the peace of God our Lord by freeing themselves from their attachment to this money, which weighs heavy on them and makes them feel uneasy. Hence they want to quiet their consciences.

Composition of Place

I will picture myself in the presence of God our Lord and all the saints, eager that I may know and desire what is most pleasing to his Divine Goodness for me.

I will ask for what I want and desire. This will be the grace to choose whatever is more for the glory of his Divine Majesty and whatever is better for the salvation of my soul.

First group The men in this first group would like to rid themselves of the attachment they have to the sum of money so that they will be able to find the peace of God our Lord and save their souls. But they never find the means to do so before the hour of death overtakes them.

Second group Those in the second group want to rid themselves of the attachment, but they wish to do so in such a way that they will keep the money. They want God to come around to what their position is. So they decide not to give up the money, not to go to God, even though a spontaneous surrender of the money would be the best course of action for them.

Third group Those who are in the third group want to rid themselves of the attachment to the money, and they want to do it in such a way that they are not inclined either to keep it or to give it up. What they want is either to hold on to it or to give it up according to whatever God our Lord will inspire them to do and what will seem to them the better decision in terms of the greater service and praise of his Divine Majesty. Moreover, men in this class see themselves as being totally unattached to either one good or another. They try not to make a choice for either one or the other until they are impelled to do so by whatever they judge to be for the greater service of God alone. As a result of this decision, their desire is to be in a position where they can better serve God our Lord. It is on this basis that they keep or give up a particular good.

I shall talk over these matters at the end of this exercise with our Lady, with Christ our Lord, and with the Father, just as I did in the Meditation on Two Standards.

Three degrees of humility: three degrees in the love of God

The Meditation on Two Standards has introduced us to the heart of the matter. We have seen how the world of its very nature is divided between good and evil, Christ and Satan, light and darkness, spirit and flesh. And so now comes the moment for the retreatant either to choose his state of life or to reform himself in the state of life he has already chosen.

In traditional spiritual language this choice is called "the election".

As a final preparation for the election process, it will be most helpful for the retreatant to look at three methods of procedure that are designed to inculcate within him a sincere love of God. St Ignatius and some other spiritual writers have designated these models the "degrees of humility". Actually, however, they are degrees of our love for God. We suggest that the retreatant reflect on them frequently during the day and that he pray peacefully the prayer recommended in the Colloquies.

The first degree or kind of humility: a humility that is necessary for salvation

It consists in this: as far as possible I subject and humble myself to the degree that I obey the law of God our Lord in all things. The result will be that I would not consider breaking any one of the commandments of God or the Church that binds under the pain of mortal sin, even if I were to gain the whole world or even if my life depended on it.

This first sort of humility is of no small importance. It describes a person who already has a sincere attachment to the will of God, an authentic degree of love for God.

The second degree of humility: better than the first

It consists in this: I have attained this state of soul when I do not look for or seek riches as opposed to poverty, or

honour rather than contempt, or a long life as opposed
to a short one, provided that the service of God and the
salvation of my soul be equally assured. With this kind of
humility I would not consider committing one venial sin,
not even for all creation, not even at the risk of saving my
life. The person who has the second degree of humility is
truly indifferent and can enjoy interior liberty, which is
indispensable in making an election. He loves God with a
very high degree of love in which, however, there is still a
trace of legalism or excessive juridical thinking.

In these first two degrees of humility it is easy to
identify the attitude of "the reasonable people" that was
described in the contemplation of the Kingdom of Christ.
Although love here is sincere and energetic, it does not yet
realise what motivates it, and therefore it does not realise
its capacity.

The third degree of humility: the most perfect humility
The third degree of humility corresponds to the love of the
insignes in the contemplation of the Kingdom.

It includes the first and second type, but it adds to them
this: in order better to imitate Christ our Lord and really
be more like him, I want and choose poverty rather than
riches; humiliations with Christ humiliated rather than
honours, supposing that the praise and glory of the Divine
Majesty be the same; and I prefer to be regarded as a man of
no account and a fool for Christ, who was the first to pass
for such, rather than be esteemed as a wise and prudent
man in this world. The person who has this disposition

goes beyond the stage of indifference; he has submitted to a personal love of Jesus Christ. This is the "*Nos stulti propter Christum*" (we are fools on Christ's account) of St Paul (*1 Co* 4:10). Let us call to mind here the "follies" of Francis of Assisi, Francis Xavier, the Curé d'Ars, etc., but let us also not forget the generosity of so many men and women who not only accept sorrows and pain and hardships in their lives but also rejoice in them because this "poverty" makes them resemble Jesus Christ all the more. Let us also call attention to the fact that if this inner disposition on the part of the retreatant is genuine and sane, it will not exclude his wanting to "cure" what is painful in his life, nor will it preclude any effort to escape from suffering. Rather, it means that if the effort proves unsuccessful, the person should rejoice that God permits him to participate so intimately in the sufferings of his Son.

Colloquies. An excellent exercise for the person who wishes to attain this third kind of humility will be to remake the three Colloquies from the Meditation on Two Standards. In these he should beg our Lord to be pleased to choose him for this third degree so that he may imitate him better and serve him more, provided that equal or greater service and praise be given to his Divine Majesty.

Sixth Day
The Last Supper

Everything is love in this stage of the Exercises; it is a love that is excessive, infinite, really altogether too much for our understanding. This is why we must accept this revelation from the heart of God and let ourselves be open to the mysteries of the Passion and death of Jesus with utmost simplicity. This comes from nothing less than complete faith in God's goodness and power. Only God can love us - can love me - to the point of suffering and dying for us - for me - in such a way.

Place yourself in God's presence and make the preparatory prayer. Ask him to inspire you.

I will call to mind the history of the mystery. Christ our Lord sent two apostles from Bethany to Jerusalem to prepare the Passover meal. Later he and the other apostles came up to join the two. After eating the paschal lamb according to the rituals prescribed by Moses, he washed the apostles' feet, instituted the Holy Eucharist, and for a long time spoke with his apostles "as one friend to another".

Composition of Place

I will see the road that leads from Bethany up to Jerusalem. Then I will imagine the Cenacle, the place where the Last Supper takes place: "an upstairs room," St Mark writes, "spacious, furnished, and all in order" (*Mk* 14:15).

I will ask for what I want and desire. Here it is sorrow, compassion, shame, because the Lord is going to his Passion for my sins.

First point: The Last Supper

I look at Jesus. He is totally aware of the symbolism of the Passover in the old law; it was simply the prefiguration of what will happen to him tonight and tomorrow. The final hour for the world has come. God's plan, wrought from pure goodness and love, "the plan he was pleased to decree in Christ", is about to be accomplished (*Ep* 1:9). Man will again "share in the glorious freedom of the children of God" (*Rm* 8:21). The world will be reconciled with God and with itself. The New Covenant will be entered into and will last forever.

Let us admire the carefulness of Christ our Lord to fulfill the Scriptures and tie in the Old Testament with the New.

Let us contemplate and feel deeply in ourselves his tremendous desire: "I have greatly desired to eat this Passover with you before I suffer" (*Lk* 22:15). What love for his Father and for us! Oh, Eucharist!

He speaks of the Kingdom of God, his Kingdom: "I tell you I shall not eat the Passover again until it is fulfilled in the Kingdom of God…. I shall not drink of the fruit of the vine until the coming of the reign of God" (*Lk* 22:16-17).

Second point: The washing of the feet

A gesture of the greatest significance because of the solemnity of the moment.

1. The Church of Jesus Christ will be a hierarchical Church, but he gives an unprecedented meaning to hierarchy, to authority:

The apostles are caught up in a dispute about the Kingdom of heaven: "An argument also began between them about who should be reckoned the greatest."

Jesus said, "No, the greatest among you must behave as if he were the youngest, the leader as if he were the one who serves" (*Lk* 22:24-26).

"Anyone among you who aspires to greatness must serve the rest" (*Mk* 10:43).

"And whoever wants to rank first among you must serve the needs of all" (*Mt* 20:27).

He himself has given the example: "Such is the case with the Son of Man who has come not to be served by others but to serve, to give his own life as a ransom for many" (*Mt* 20:28).

Now he joins what he says with what he does: "He rose from the meal and took off his cloak. He picked up the towel and tied it around himself. Then he poured water into a basin and began to wash his disciples' feet and dry them with the towel he had around him" (*Jn* 13:4-5).

What a revolution in the concept of a community and the role played by its chief and leader!

2. The conversation between Judas and Peter:

Yes, Jesus has washed the feet of Judas. With what tenderness and consideration! He has already stated on a number of occasions that he was aware of Judas' intentions.

But the traitor set his face against him. Finally, Jesus told him, "Be quick about what you are to do", and Judas left. In reporting the scene St John uses an astounding expression: "It was night". Night! Outside, or in the heart of the traitor (*Jn* 13:17-30)?

Jesus also washes the feet of Peter. At first Peter refuses: "Never! You shall never wash my feet." Jesus had to convince him with a decisive argument: "If I do not wash you, you can have no share with me." (*Mecum!*) And Peter gives the response of the insignes: "Well, then, Lord, not only my feet but my hands and my head as well!" (*Jn* 13:6-8). To be with Jesus one must be ready to be with him all the way. Generous Peter is, but not sinless!

Third Point: Jesus institutes the Eucharist and
the priesthood

1. Let us reread the admirable account of what takes place next, either in 1 Corinthians 11:17-30, to which we should add 1 Corinthians 10:16-17, or in one of the Synoptics (*Lk* 22; *Mk* 14; *Mt* 26) - or the words of the canons in our missal.

In order to understand the correct and literal sense of the Eucharist, it would be good to reread chapter 6 in St John's Gospel: "I am the bread of life. No one who comes to me will ever hunger; no one who believes in me will ever thirst…It is my Father's will that whoever sees the Son and believes in him should have eternal life and that I should raise that person up on the Last Day…and the bread I shall give is my flesh, for the life of the world…Whoever eats my flesh and drinks my blood lives in me, and I live in that person." Now listen to those who hear him on this occasion murmur, see them walking away…and repeat with St Peter, "Lord, to whom shall we go? You have the message of eternal life, and we believe."

2. The whole structural meaning of the Old Testament is summed up here (*Heb* 8 to 10). The priesthood comes into being.

3. Let us meditate with feeling on John's expression: "He had loved his own in the world and would show his love for them to the end" (*Jn* 13:1). "*Infinem dilexit eos*": He loved them to the end, to the extremity of his infinite love. This is how he loved me: *Dilexit me.*
Infinem: to the end.

• Here is where the Incarnation and the thematic development of his love reach their fulfilment.

• Here is where the self-abasement of Christ our Lord is realised. The eucharistic state!

• Here the redemption is accomplished because through the Eucharist Christ promises to go to the limits of the Passion, all the way to the Resurrection.

• Here is fulfilled the Mosaic law and here begins (reaches its completion) the new law. Jesus will soon begin his "last discourse" with the new commandment of fraternal charity, and he will develop God's new plan, the "restored" plan "*mirabilis reformasti*".

- Here the "*sint unum*" - that they may be one - of the priestly prayer reaches completion. Through the Eucharist the Church is already established.

And everything the Eucharist means for Christ, it means for the priest.

How the Divinity hides itself. "Oh, hidden God, I adore you!" I will converse with Christ our Lord. Many things I have to talk to him about here: adoration, faith, thanksgiving. May what he asked for in his "last discourse" and his "sacerdotal prayer" be realised through me.

———

I will end my contemplation with the *Our Father*. What meaning the Lord's prayer takes on here, in the upper room, this evening!

The Seventh Day
The Agony in the Garden

Every event that takes place during the Passion actually encompasses all the other events. For this reason let us follow more closely than ever before St Ignatius' advice: "I will remain quietly meditating upon the point in which I have found what I desire, without any eagerness to go on until I have been satisfied."

Place yourself in the presence of God and make the prayer beginning the meditation. Ask him to inspire you.

I will recall first of all the history of what is covered in this meditation. Christ our Lord went down from Mount Zion (where he had eaten the Last Supper with his twelve apostles) towards the Valley of Jehoshaphat, and then up towards the Garden of Olives. He leaves eight of the apostles just outside the Garden; the remaining three - Peter, James and John - he brings with him into the Garden.

Then, leaving these three, he goes more deeply into the olive groves, where he begins to pray. During his prayer his sweat becomes like drops of blood. After having prayed three times to his Father, he wakes up the three disciples. His enemies make their appearance, Judas leading them on. Judas gives him a kiss of peace. St Peter cuts off the ear of Malchus, and Jesus heals the wound. They arrest him as if he were a bandit. Next they drag him down to the valley and then up the opposite hill to Jerusalem and to the house of Annas.

Composition of Place

See the two roads. The first is the short road going from Mount Zion down to the valley of Jehoshaphat. From the valley rise up two hills. On the slopes of the eastern one is the Mount of Olives. It faces the western hill, where Mount Zion is located and where, behind, the walls of Jerusalem are visible. Then there is the road from the walls to the house of Annas.

I will ask for what I want and desire. Here it is proper to ask for sorrow with Christ in sorrow, anguish with Christ in anguish, interior grief because of the great sufferings Christ endures for me.

First point: What is at stake in the struggle of Christ our Lord

What is at stake is his "glorious freedom as a Son of God", the filial adherence of his will to the will of the Father, his love, his total and definitive Yes to the Father.

Here Jesus is faced with the essential act that must be accomplished to complete the Father's plan of love, the plan the prophets prophesied without fully understanding its meaning: "They investigated the times and the circumstances that the Spirit of Christ within them was pointing to, for he predicted the sufferings destined for Christ and the glories that would follow" (1 Pet 1:11). This is the profound mystery the angels watched in astonishment. Jesus is alone during his struggle. When he arrived in Gethsemane, he told his eight apostles, "Stay here while I go over there to pray". A little later he said to Peter, James and John, "Wait here and stay awake with me" (*Mt* 26:37-39). A terrible sense of loneliness. He will scarcely be able to stand it; three times he will return to those who were supposed to watch with him…they slept… yes, indeed, he is alone, completely alone!

He sees before him the world of sin, and he sees also divine love, misunderstood and scorned…sins of every age…sins of every person. Or better: he sees sinful human nature, torn away from the Father, enslaved to the "Prince of Darkness".

He feels the malice, the total perversity of this sin in the world - this evil that we cannot grasp with our reason and that goes far beyond our understanding - but he is able to measure it against the Father's overabundant love because he has always known the heart of the Father.

He knows that only an excessive redemption (his Passion) or an excessive punishment (hell) could correspond to his Father's excessive love. He was caught up in this awesome dilemma; and now the hour has come for him to decide, to choose once and for all. Or rather, as St Paul says, because he is the Yes to all the Father's promises, the hour is come for him to ratify his mission (*1 Co* 1:20).

"My heart is nearly broken with sorrow" (*Mt* 26:38). He was afraid. Fright and dejection pour into his soul. Feel, ponder and mull over this "desolation" of the Son of God. Indeed, with the exception of sin itself, he was truly clothed "in the same sinful flesh" as ourselves (*Rm* 8:3).

And the drama of his choice was that it had repercussions throughout his flesh.

Even to the point that he sweat blood: "And his sweat became like drops of blood falling to the ground" (*Lk* 22:44). "This supposes", comments St Ignatius, "that his garments were saturated with blood."

During this agony he is tempted: tempted as he was before by Satan in the desert, tempted to give up, to forget it all. "Abba [O Father], you have the power to do all things. Take this cup away from me!" (*Mk* 14:36). Contemplate to what extent Jesus must be dejected, oppressed, to let such words escape from his filial lips. What disgust, what bitterness! We should observe that he did not revolt against his Father's will; he simply desired that that will would change.

At this point of his temptation, one word would change everything. He had cried out, "Abba [O Father]!" This is not a cry of revolt or hopeless resignation; it is the cry of a son, a cry of confidence in the Father at the height of his suffering, a cry that is already acceptance. In that word "Abba" there is already contained all of the "*non mea voluntas, sed tua fiat*" - that is, all of the meaning contained in the prayer "But let it be as you would have it, not as I."

Three times he came back to see his apostles. They were sleeping. Three times he returned to his place of prayer: "Going back again, he began to pray in the same words" (*Mk* 14:39); "Father, if it is your will, take this cup from me; yet not my will but yours be done" (*Lk* 22:42).

Love came out the victor from this agony of Christ. "Liberty" triumphed. "The Father and I are one" of the priestly prayer is affirmed here in the Person of Christ our

Lord. In him our sinful flesh becomes a flesh of obedience and filial fidelity.

Second point: Jesus' prayer

This prayer of Jesus at Gethsemane can be considered as the pattern for prayer, the model of all prayer, the prayer that goes beyond all methods.

1. Indeed, to some extent the drama of the redemption must always be operative at the heart of every prayer: our own personal drama, inseparable from who we are, but which we must live with Jesus Christ.

Let us pay particular attention to what St Luke says when Jesus leaves the upper room on Holy Thursday night: "He then left to make his way as usual to the Mount of Olives, with his disciples following" (*Lk* 22:39). His agony this night had been preceded by other "agonies".

2. In this drama of prayer we are accompanied by our temptations and contradictions, by our outbursts of generosity and our moments of selfishness, by our acts of submission and our movements of revolt, by our times of peace and our moments of distress. Just like Jesus, who both desired this hour and had a disgust and horror of it, let us not be surprised by the wavering of our own will. It is part of the work of redemption. A person can be "desolate and tempted to run off" and at the same time love and say Yes to our Father.

3. This personal drama has to play itself out in our prayer. The circumstances of who we are, what we do and what is

in store for us in the future (our activities, sufferings, joys, failures, etc.) - all of these we have to bear. At the same time, we bear them all in our personal conscience and in our conscience as Christians; that is, we bear all of these as men who participate with Christ in the redemption of the world.

4. Father - this is the word that saves all - which necessarily is *"Ita, Pater"* ("Yes, Father"). The importance and the beauty in our lives of the prayer the *Our Father*…its place at the heart of our deepest being…it is here at Gethsemane that Jesus teaches us to say this prayer.

5. Let us be humble, as Jesus was humble, in this combat that is our prayer. He, the Son of God, calls for and accepts the comfort of the angel. The angel is the sign of the love of the Father. Let us look for and accept everything that can assist us in our prayer. Such is the prayer of the poor man! Such is the prayer of the publican! Such is the prayer of the Canaanite woman!

6. If our prayer is a redemptive prayer, we should not be surprised if it wanders here and there and that we are always repeating the same words. At Gethsemane Jesus comes and goes; he looks for support and does not find it, but, as St Mark tells us, "Going back again he began to pray in the same words" (14:39). A love without words…a prayer more real than the most beautiful formulas ever composed.

7. Despite his personal agony, Jesus thinks of others, of his apostles: "Be on guard and pray that you may not undergo the test" (*Mt* 26:41). "And lead us not into temptation."

8. Savour the contrast of the tragic prayer at Gethsemane with the energetic "Get up! Let us be on our way!" that he says as Judas and the cohort come into the Garden (*Mt* 26:46). Strength: that is what comes from redemptive prayer. The Virgin Mary, the coredemptrix, stood near the Cross of Jesus (*Jn* 19:25).

Third point: The Apostles run off

The sequel to all of the events that occurred up to the time of his capture takes place before the Passion, when his body is mutilated. It comes about now in the passion that rips apart his human heart - that is, when his own ran off abandoning him, forsaking him.

"With that, all deserted him and fled", reports St Mark (14:50).

Think about how sad that word "all" is.

All, even Peter, the fighter.

All, even John, "the disciple whom Jesus loved".

All? No, over there is his Mother. She shows compassion for him. But for him, his Mother's compassion means an increase of suffering.

All? No, Judas is there, too. He gives him the only sign of friendship this night - a kiss. But this particular kiss is the sign of treason. Jesus does not shirk from Judas' kiss, but think about how bitter it is for him. Consider the infinite sadness in his complaint: "Friend, do what you are here for!" (*Mt* 26:50).

I will close my contemplation by conversing about these matters with Christ our Lord, who goes to his Passion for my sins: "He poured out for you every drop of his blood" (Pascal). After watching Peter flee and John run off, dare I pose here the questions I asked myself in the Colloquy of Mercy (see pp.19-23): "What will I do for Christ? What should I do for Christ?" After seeing the kiss of friendship perverted - "Friend, a kiss…?" - dare I talk with him "as one friend to another"?

In my confusion I will catch up with Peter: Peter "following him from afar" and who will deny him, but who will immediately weep over his treachery. This then is the irony of that grace I have prayed for on the Fifth Day: "So that I may imitate him better and follow him more closely". On this Holy Thursday evening in the company of Peter I feel I have the companionship I need. I am…far off; but I do follow him, and that in itself is already something!

Then I will meet up with our Lady and ask her for her heart, her tears, to *com patī*, to "suffer with" Jesus in his distress as he goes to his Passion.

I will conclude with the *Our Father*.

The Via Dolorosa: Jesus at the house of Caiaphas and before the Sanhedrin

Place yourself in the presence of God and make the prayer that begins the meditation. Ask him to inspire you.

I will call to mind the history of the events. Jesus' hands are bound, and he is dragged from the Garden of Olives to the house of Annas (the father-in-law of the High Priest Caiaphas). But Annas sends him back to Caiaphas (*Jn*

18:24). Peter is there and denies his Master three times. Meanwhile, until daybreak, when the Sanhedrin will meet, Jesus is insulted, taunted and slapped by his guards. Morning arrives, and the elders of the people, the chief priests, and the scribes meet together in the council of the Sanhedrin.

They condemn Jesus to death. Judas, in despair, hangs himself. After passing sentence, Caiaphas has Jesus sent to Pilate, the Roman governor, who alone has the power to pronounce the death penalty.

Composition of Place

I will see the house of the High Priest Caiaphas with its courtyard where his retainers are warming their hands and where Peter comes and sits down…with its guardhouse where Jesus is manhandled, brutalised…and with its grand hall where the Sanhedrin meets and where Jesus is condemned for having said he is the "Son of God".

I will ask for what I want and desire. Here it will be sorrow with Christ in sorrow, anguish with Christ in anguish, interior grief for so much suffering that Christ endures for me.

First point: Peter's triple denial

1. I am in the inner court of Caiaphas' house. In one corner is Jesus. He is all tied up and used by the guards as if he were something to spit at. They also beat him up and taunt him. Then, covering his eyes, they strike him: "Prophesy! Who struck you?" In another corner a fire is burning.

Servants and soldiers are sitting around it warming their hands. Peter comes up, and he sits down, too. He is full of remorse for having run off when Jesus was arrested. Follow the events as they are presented by Mark (14:54-73).

2. The atmosphere around the fire lends itself to easy conversation: "You too were with Jesus of Nazareth." Peter denies it: "I do not even know the man you are talking about!" What irony!

3. Then Jesus turns and looks at Peter (*Lk* 22:61). Contemplate that look. Peter gets up and leaves. He cries bitterly. Reflect on Peter's tears.

Second point: Jesus before Caiaphas and the Sanhedrin

1. The Sanhedrin looked for testimony to bring against Jesus. But the witnesses succeeded only in contradicting themselves. At last, one of them recalled that Jesus had said, "I shall destroy this temple made by human hands, and in three days I will construct another not made by human hands" (see *Mk* 14:58).

2. Finally, the high priest asked him, "Are you the Messiah, the Son of the Blessed One?" And Jesus answered, "I am, and you will see the Son of Man seated at the right hand of the Power and coming with the clouds of heaven."

3. The high priest tore his robes and said, "What further need do we have of witnesses? You have heard the blasphemy. What is your verdict?" And they all condemned him to death (*Mk* 14:63-64).

Third point: Judas

1. Then Judas, seeing that Jesus was condemned, repented. Think about the despair contained in that repentance.

2. He brought back the thirty pieces of silver, the price of his treasonous act. The chief priests and elders refused to accept it. What a complicated predicament the traitor has created for himself! Does this make him repent? Does he now turn interiorly towards Jesus? Or does he despair?

3. Judas throws the thirty pieces of silver on the temple floor and then goes out and hangs himself.

Consider and try to appreciate the traitor's loss of hope; such a heavy weight brooded over his soul. What a difference between his attitude and that of Peter!

I will converse with Christ our Lord, offended and condemned for my sins. I will adore him. I will say to him what the priest prays just before Communion at Mass: "Never let me be parted from you." I will ask him that, if ever I should be so evil as to betray him, I may shed the tears of Peter rather than give in to the despair of Judas.

I will end the meditation with the *Our Father*.

The Via Dolorosa: From Pilate's praetorium to Calvary

What happens here is beyond all words. Each person will follow where grace bids him to go so as "to enter" intimately into the mystery of Christ's death.

Here are three suggestions. The retreatant may want to select one or another among them as he desires.

1. Read over slowly, peacefully, lovingly - with the attitude one has when he assists at the Mass or reads the office of Good Friday - the whole Passion from one of the four evangelists.

St Ignatius would have approved using the *lectio divina* here. He gives the following advice to the retreatant who "wishes to spend more time on the Passion": "When he finishes the Passion [that is, taking mystery after mystery for the subject of his contemplation], he may devote one whole day to the consideration of the first half of the Passion and a second day to the other half and a third day to the whole Passion."

2. Make a lengthy, deeply contemplative Way of the Cross. It should be very personal. See the events clearly as they are, in their tragic reality.

3. Listen to, ponder over, reflect upon the Seven Words of Christ on the Cross:

- "Father, forgive them; they do not know what they are doing."

- "Today you will be with me in paradise."

- "Woman, there is your son. This is your mother."

- "My God, my God, why have you forsaken me?"

- "I am thirsty."

- "Now it is finished."

- "Father, into your hands I commend my spirit."

Whatever choice one would make, he could enhance the reality of the contemplation by choosing one or more of these options:

• Reading St Paul's account of the gradual self-abasement of the Word of God (*Phil* 2:6-11).

• Reflecting on the passage from Galatians (2:20) about the "Son of God, who loved me and gave himself for me".

• Renewing the Colloquy of Mercy (see pp. 19-23).

• Reconsidering the meditations on the call of the king and the Two Standards;

• Implementing in my day-to-day attitudes the recommendations St Ignatius gives to those making this retreat:

> • "To consider what Christ our Lord suffers in his human nature; to do all in my power to suffer and be sad for him."

> • "To consider how the Divinity hides itself; for example, it could annihilate its enemies, yet it does not do so but leaves the most sacred humanity to endure so many cruel sufferings."

> • "To consider how our Lord suffers so much for my sins and what I ought to do and to suffer for him."

This whole contemplation ought to be a conversation, a friendly colloquy with my Saviour, and most especially it should be a "simple looking at", a "pure consideration".

The Passion makes its appeal to faith and the heart, not to words. It is a mystery of love before which I simply allow myself to be so that, imperceptibly and gradually, I can be drawn more deeply into its depths.

I will again end my prayer with the Our Father - this time at the foot of the Cross where the words take on an extraordinary meaning. I shall also repeat word by word the prayer *Soul of Christ* (*Anima Christi*).

The solitude of Our Lady

As I complete these contemplations on the great mystery of the Passion of Christ our Lord, I shall consider, by way of a repetition, the solitude experienced by Our Lady on Good Friday evening and during the course of the following day. Many people have used this "Holy Saturday spirituality" as a way to God. The ancient Fathers recommended our reminding God of Jesus and what he did for each and all of us as an excellent method of prayer.

Place yourself in the presence of God and make the prayer beginning the contemplation. Ask him to inspire you.

I will call to mind the history of the events. Our Lady was present with Jesus on his way to Calvary. She stood near the Cross. Jesus told his Mother that John was now her son while giving his beloved disciple his Mother. There was the descent from the Cross. Afterwards Jesus was placed in the tomb. Then she went home with John. Mary is the most perfect model of the "*Mecum*", that is, the "with me"; she indeed is the one who had "compassion", "suffered with", her Son. In the eyes of the crowd who put him to death, she was the mother of "the Imposter", the mother of the one who was condemned. And in the eyes of God?

Composition of Place

In a little private room in the place where John was housed.

I will ask for what I want and desire. Here it will be a heart to "empathise" - that is, to "feel within" me what Jesus Christ feels.

First point: The solitude of Our Lady between the Passion and the Resurrection

1. The cause for this terrible solitude: "he" is no longer here:

He, her Son! She watched over him as a small baby. Then there was Bethlehem…Nazareth…his farewell to her before beginning his public life…Cana. All of these things she "kept in her heart", and particularly those events she witnessed during the Passion.

She contemplates "the sufferings, pains, and anguish that Christ our Lord endured from the time of his birth down to Calvary", just as St Ignatius asks us to consider them.

The sword of sorrow, predicted by Simeon, pierced her soul. She is the one who knows who Jesus truly is because she is the one who lives out fully the drama of our redemption. And she reconciles this drama perfectly within her own soul. Like Jesus during his agony in the Garden, her response is also, "Yes, Father."

2. Even though full of sorrow, hers was a faith-filled, hope-filled solitude:

Stabat Mater: Mary stood beneath the Cross, her faith intact.

Her faith never knew the fluctuation and hesitations of the faith of the apostles.

Her Son no longer suffers. The pain-filled phase of the redemption is finished: "For your faithful people life is changed, not ended", as the Preface of the Mass of the Dead tells us.

She knows the Resurrection is certain and that it is near. She remembers the words of Jesus announcing his Resurrection - and that "that imposter while he was still alive made the claim, 'After three days I will rise'" (*Mt* 27:63). And that he will rebuild the temple (of his body) in three days.

She further recalled, "And I - once I am lifted up from earth - will draw all men to myself" (*Jn* 12:32). Yes, that day was already dawning. It began at Calvary: there were the good thief, the centurion, and those who "went home beating their breasts" (*Lk* 23:48). The realisation of all of this did not stave off her grief as a mother, yet the joy of charity gave some perspective to her sorrow.

It was because of this certitude that her anguish, even though not diminished, was nevertheless appeased. Spend a long time reflecting on Our Lady's serenity, on this quiet peace.

3. Her solitude, however, was filled up by the presence of the Holy Trinity:

Her unity with the Trinity was, of course, never interrupted. But today that unity is more centred, more intense. The "beneficent plan" of the Father is realised. The Annunciation is accomplished: "I am the servant of the Lord. Let it be done to me as you say" (*Lk* 1:38). How far-reaching are certain words in the world's destiny!

The Son. Think about how he said, "My Mother"! It was with the same resonance, the same tenderness that he said, "My Father" - that is, in the Holy Spirit. Without her the redemption would have been impossible. Because of her Immaculate Conception she benefited in an exceptional way in the Son's redemption, and therefore he rejoiced in her, the first of his redeemed.

The Holy Spirit, to whom she was always perfectly disposed. He now wants her to assist in his future enterprise - that is, in creating the Church, in being the soul of his soul.

Spend a long time savouring this solitude, this silence, this simplicity of Our Lady. How beautiful, how wonderful it is!

Second point: Our Lady's solitude is open to the apostles who return

Because they too are "alone". But their loneliness is of a completely different type from Mary's solitude. Their solitude is the aloneness of the sinner, of him "who would deserve to be reprimanded and considered fainthearted", as we considered in the meditation on the call of the King. The solitude of those like the disciples on their way to Emmaus, "who had hoped", and who were disappointed by the events that had taken place, and who had seen their dreams shattered. The solitude of sterility and desolation. How bitter!

Mary welcomes John. She was living where he was lodged. He had been with her at Calvary: "Woman, there is your son" (*Jn* 19:26). By privileged title, from that moment on, he is her son. He mourns the death of a friend, and what a Friend…a Brother in Mary!

She welcomes the turncoat Peter. She reminds him: "You are Peter, and on this rock, he will build his Church…. He had predicted that you would deny him three times before the cock crowed, but once converted, you would strengthen your brothers…Be up and about now, Peter. The time has come for you to give them courage." She taught him humility, the beautiful, holy by-product of sin. It was from Mary that Peter learned to rely no longer on himself ("Peter, do you love me?") but on Jesus alone, who knew him and who would give him confidence ("Lord, you know that I love you").

She welcomes the other apostles. They had believed themselves so strong, and yet they all ran off, all of them. Now, one by one, they return. She would love to welcome even Judas, to pardon him, and to remind him of the many, many times he had seen her Son extend pardon to others. She would tell him, "He loves you, and he gave himself up for you. *Dilexit te*." And she would also say, "The one who was pardoned the most is the one who is loved the most."

Undoubtedly Mary Magdalene also came to see Our Lady. And Martha, and Mary of Bethany. And Lazarus, whom Jesus raised from the dead.

With courtesy and affection she communicated to all of these her peace, her faith, and her hope. She initiates the role of "the comforter", a role that the resurrected Jesus will so magnificently exercise. It is a role that is not by any means mere play acting but one in which the person gives only what he truly "has" and what he really "is".

Rest awhile in a corner of that room, listening, watching, contemplating, admiring.

Third point: The Church is already begun in the very heart of Christ's failure

Yes, that is so, thanks to this woman full of grief but with her faith intact.

It is with faith-filled grief that she gathers together Jesus' friends, one after the other. On Easter morning the regroupment will be complete. It is a sparse and humble band - like the "remnant of Israel" of old, like so many grains of wheat buried in the ground, where the "power of God" will have them sprout forth a harvest.

This will be the group associated with the Resurrection, the Ascension and Pentecost, the very first Christian community. And so the Church is planted in the world, a group of true friends of Jesus who believe in his Resurrection!

And here is an admirable thing to reflect upon: at the same time that she renounces her precious solitude to give birth to the Church, Our Lady discovers another solitude, another silence in the Church: "Peter, it is you who will command, govern, and rule. You are Peter." The Acts of the

Apostles will mention her again, but very seldom. Nothing about the risen Jesus' apparition to his Mother, nothing about her life, nothing about her death. In Christian Tradition there will be two places of the "Dormition of the Virgin", one at Jerusalem, the other at Ephesus. Silence, solitude, but she is at the very heart of the living Church.

After fulfilling her historic role as Redemptrix, she will begin here her role as Mediatrix, the Mother of every Christian.

———◦◦◦———

I also will converse with our Lady, begging her to pardon me for having betrayed her Son, confiding to her, in spite of my wretchedness, that I still desire to love and to imitate her Son: "Hail, Mother of mercy"; "Pray for us sinners!"

I will end my prayer with the *Our Father*.

Eighth Day
The Resurrection and the Appearances
of the Risen Christ

First of all, here are a few recommendations St Ignatius gives us to create the atmosphere of the last section of the *Spiritual Exercises*.

"As soon as I awaken, I shall place before my mind the scene I am about to contemplate; I shall seek to stir up in myself the joy and happiness of Christ our Lord, and I shall endeavour to find enjoyment in thinking about it."

"I will think about subjects that stimulate happiness, cheerfulness, and spiritual joy, such as the glory of heaven."

"I shall make use of the sunshine of the day, of the pleasures of the season, etc., insofar as my soul esteems that all of these things may help it rejoice in its Creator and in its Redeemer."

Place yourself in God's presence and make the prayer that begins the meditation.

Ask him to inspire you.

I will call to mind the history of the events in this mystery. The exact account of the event itself is found nowhere in the Gospels. Where we have the proof of the Resurrection are in the empty tomb, in the unquestionable testimony of the holy women who went to the sepulchre early in the morning carrying spices, and in the experience of Peter and John. In addition to these there were the appearances of the risen Christ during the course of the next forty days that would give the Resurrection its true significance (see St Paul's stated case in *1 Co* 15:1-11).

Composition of Place

The tomb in the Church of the Holy Sepulchre at Jerusalem or before some tomb in the countryside. In front of it there is a massive, heavy, round rock that is used to seal the entrance.

I will ask for what I want and desire. Here it is the grace of experiencing intense gladness and joy because of the great glory and joy of Christ our Lord.

During the last part of the *Spiritual Exercises*, St Ignatius advises us:

1. to consider how the Divinity, which seemed to hide itself during the Passion, now appears and reveals itself so wonderfully in the holy Resurrection.

2. to spend some time admiring the role of consoler that Christ our Lord plays. He acts just like ordinary friends do when they want to console one another: "He loved me."

First point: The empty tomb

"'Jesus of Nazareth is not here, for he has risen, as he said he would'" (*Mt* 28:6).

Let us take our place among the group of apostles and disciples who cluster about Our Lady on Easter morning. Most probably they are at John's house. (We are not going to try to orchestrate the various apparitions according to when and where they took place because the Gospel accounts offer no such arrangement. Rather, what we are going to do for the most part is follow the account found in John's Gospel [20:1-31], because John is an exact witness, telling us what he saw. His witness is supported by Luke [24:12], who in turn received his account from Peter, another witness to the events.)

In the morning, "while it was still dark", the women, carrying their spices, left for the tomb of Christ. They did not perform these burial rites the day before because they observed the sabbath as a day of rest. These women were Mary Magdalene, Joanna, and Mary the mother of James. Let us accompany them as they make their way along the road. "Who will roll back the stone for us from the entrance to the tomb?" (*Mk* 16:3). But when they arrive at their destination they find the stone rolled aside and the tomb opened and empty.

Mary Magdalene runs off to alert Peter and "the other disciple (the one Jesus loved)". She reports, "The Lord has been taken from the tomb! We do not know where they have put him."

However, the other women, who had stayed close by the sepulchre, entered the tomb, where they saw "a young man" (according to Mark and Matthew, but "two young men", according to Luke) dressed in white who said to them, "There is no need to be so amazed.... Why do you search for the Living One among the dead? You are looking for Jesus of Nazareth; he has been raised up. Remember what he said to you while he was still in Galilee - that the Son of Man must be delivered into the hands of sinful men and be crucified and on the third day rise again.... See, here is the place where they laid him" (*Lk* 24:5-7; *Mk* 16:6). The women made their way out of the tomb bewildered and trembling because "they were frightened out of their wits" (*Mk* 16:8).

When Peter learns the news from Mary Magdalene, he takes John with him and runs off to the sepulchre. John is the first to arrive but does not enter the tomb. Peter arrives and goes in. There he sees the burial wrappings and the piece of cloth that had covered the face and head of the dead Jesus. He saw "the piece of cloth that had covered the head not lying with the wrappings, but rolled up in a place by itself" (*Jn* 20:7). Then John enters the tomb: "He saw and believed." The two disciples return home. Finally, sometime during the day Jesus appears to Peter (*Lk* 24:34).

Mary Magdalene had remained in the vicinity of the tomb. Now she is crying. Jesus appears to her: "Woman, why are you weeping? Who is it that you are looking for?" She takes him for the gardener and says, "Sir, if you are the one who carried him off, tell me where you have put him, and I will go and remove him"…"*Maryam*"…"*Rabbouni*" (*Jn* 20:11-19).

What confusion there is now among his faithful followers in Jerusalem! Joy is mixed with apprehension! What is the meaning of all of this? We get some inkling of the uneasiness in the words of the disciples who were making their way to Emmaus on that Sunday afternoon: "Some of the women of our group have just brought us some astonishing news," they say. "They were at the tomb before dawn and failed to find his body but returned with the tale that they had seen a vision of angels who declared he was alive. Some of our number went to the tomb and found it to be just as the women said, but they did not see him" (*Lk* 24:22-24). The confusion becomes more widespread throughout Jerusalem. The Sanhedrin order the men guarding the tomb to get the word around that the disciples have stolen the body.

Relive this Easter morning. Appreciate the fear of Jesus' friends and their progressive growth in faith, hope, and love.

Second point: The Resurrection and Christian faith

Reread St Paul's beautiful text in 1 Corinthians 15:12-26.

The totality of our Christian belief rests on our faith in the Resurrection of Jesus: "If Christ has not been raised, our preaching is void of content, and your faith is empty, too…. If our hopes in Christ are limited to this life only, we are the most pitiable of men."

When the apostles first went out to preach the Gospel message, they made the death and Resurrection of Jesus the pivotal point of their message (the kerygma). Read Peter's five discourses (Acts 2, 3, 10, etc.) and Paul's sermon in Acts 13.

It is in the Resurrection that we find the essence of our Faith, the epicentre of the Creed. One day we too shall rise with a body similar to that of the risen Christ (see *1 Co* 15:35-38).

Third point: The Resurrection and Christian life

Reread once more the text describing "the kenosis" (*Phil* 2:6-11) while keeping in mind the introductory words in verse 5: "Make your own the mind of Christ Jesus." This is what Christian life means (see *Ep* 5:1-2: imitate God… follow the way of love, that is, live in love, in the same way as Christ who loved us).

This whole process begins with our baptism (*Rm* 6:1-11), and the rest of our Christian life consists of participating at each moment, each day, in the mystery of Christ's death and Resurrection. "I am resurrected with Christ." I must convince myself of that reality. I must place that reality at the heart of my being, at the core of my work, at the centre of my relations with all those with whom I come in contact. It must colour my vision of the world. What a change in my thinking this way of looking at things will make! What dynamic energy it will give to my life, to how I see myself and others, to what I do, to how I view the world!

It is here that we find "the glorious freedom as children of God". He liberates us, and with us he liberates all of creation (*Rm* 8:12-24).

In ending this contemplation I will converse intimately:

  • with the risen Jesus… reliving with him the marvellous scenes of his apparitions;

  • with Our Lady, asking her for her faith;

  • with one or another of the apostles: Peter… John… I will conclude with an *Our Father*.

Concluding Meditation
Contemplation To Attain and Live
in the Love of God

This contemplation summarises, as it were, the whole of the *Spiritual Exercises.* It provides the retreatant, who will shortly be going back to his regular schedule, with a basically spiritual way of looking at things, a vision of the world, a solid, simple spirituality that he can implement each day at his work or in dealing with the problems of life he has to face. The permanent setting of the "celestial court" where St Ignatius now situates the retreatant; the simple yet demanding law of "love for love" that now supersedes the "praise, reverence, and serve God our Lord" of the Foundation part of the Exercises; the most humble and filial concept of "abandonment", which now takes the place of difficult concepts contained in the Exercises, like indifference and election; all this realism of faith and nature, this fusion of spirit and action in the same movement of life - all of these features make the Contemplation to Attain Love of God the synthesis of Christian life. It is the Foundation all over again, if one wishes to put it that way, but now it is the Foundation lived out in every phase of one's life, from the most commonplace to the most adventuresome. Christian life is a relationship of permanent love between the Father, who is in heaven, and his Son, who lives on earth in men and in creation. "In him we live and move and have our being… for we too are his offspring" (*Ac* 17:28).

St Ignatius recommended that before beginning this Exercise, it would be good to call attention to these two points:

1. Love ought to manifest itself in deeds rather than in words.

2. Love consists in a mutual sharing of goods. The person who loves communicates to his beloved all or part of what he has, and likewise the beloved with the lover. Hence, if one has knowledge, he shares it with the one who does not have it; the same goes for honours or riches. And thus there is always a mutual giving and receiving.

Such are the fundamental laws of love or of true friendship. Place yourself in the presence of God and the whole celestial court, the angels and saints, just as in the Preface of the Mass when we are invited to do so by joining with the choirs of heaven to sing "Holy, Holy, Holy".

And this is not a simple composition of place; this is a permanent reality.

Make the prayer beginning the contemplation and ask God to inspire you.

I will ask for what I want and desire. Here this will be an intimate knowledge of the many and wonderful gifts I have received from God, so that in return, filled with gratitude, I may love and serve his Divine Majesty in all things.

"Lord, give me new eyes, a new heart, so that henceforth I shall be able to see the heavens and earth as the new heavens and the new earth, as was promised by your Word to those in whom your Spirit of love would dwell."

First point: Love is a gift, a continuous mutual exchange of all that one has and is

God has given to me all that I possess: the gift of creation, redemption, and my particular personal gifts.

With much love I shall take into account how much our Lord has done for me, how much he has given me of what he has: "O Divine Goodness".

Through his grace, he has even given me what he is. According to his divine plan, he gives himself to me as much as he possibly can.

I will reflect now for a moment on myself. According to all reason and justice, I for my part ought to offer his Divine Majesty all the good things that I have and myself along with them. And this I ought to do as one moved by an outburst of great love. For this reason I ought to say to him:

> Take, Lord, and receive all my liberty,
> my memory, my understanding, and my entire will,
>   all that I have and possess.
> You have given all to me.
> To you, Lord, I return it.
> All is yours:
> Dispose of it wholly according to your will.
> Give me your love and your grace; this is sufficient for me.

Second point: Love is reciprocal, being present to the other at each moment

I will look at how God dwells in his creatures, in material beings, giving them existence; in plants, giving them life;

in animals, giving them sensation; in men, giving them understanding through their intellect.

So he dwells in me, giving me existence, life, sensation, intelligence.

More than this, he has made me his temple, first of all by creating me "in his image and likeness", but especially by dwelling within me through the grace of my baptism.

Then I will reflect on myself. According to all reason and justice I ought on my part to endeavour to live in God ("to live in": an expression dear to the Apostle St John), to make my dwelling place in him, to make him present to me at every moment and me present to him, so that I belong to him completely. And I will then renew my offering as one who would make an offering moved by an outburst of great love: "Take, Lord, and receive…"

Third point: Love is a total sharing in every activity

I will consider how God works and labours for me and for all creatures on the face of the earth. He conducts himself as one who prepares and disposes everything for the one he loves.

More than this, he works and labours in me by giving me everything that I have so that I myself can work and labour - and especially he works in me through his grace, giving my work an infinite effectiveness. The result is that in some way my life is divinised.

I will then reflect on myself. According to all reason and justice, I for my part ought to work and labour for God, giving myself entirely to his service and his glory and showing his Divine Majesty all the good and helpful things I do in the place here on earth where his Providence has placed me. And I will renew my offering as one would do moved by an outburst of great love: "Take, Lord, and receive…"

Fourth point: In love we belong to each other, we partake of what is ours

Just as all rays shine forth from the sun, as waters gush from the spring, so do all that is good and every gift I have come from God: my limited power from his infinite and sovereign power, my limited goodness from his goodness; my piety from his holiness, my compassion from his compassion, etc.

Especially, the grace in me comes to me as a gratuitous gift from his divine life.

I shall reflect on myself. According to all reason and justice, I for my part ought to attach myself to the Source and open myself completely to Divine Influence so that there is nothing that encumbers or dilutes his radiant activity in me. And I shall repeat once again my offering, as someone who makes an offering moved by an outburst of great love: "Take, Lord, and receive…"

What a transformation this makes of my whole life here below! I can at last realise this wonderful ideal that God from the very beginning proposed to man: "Hear, O Israel! The Lord is our God, the Lord alone! Therefore, you shall love the Lord, your God, with all your heart, and with all your soul, and with all your strength. Take to heart these words that I enjoin on you today. Drill them into your children. Speak of them at home and abroad, whether you are busy or at rest. Bind them onto your wrist as a sign and let them be as a pendant on your forehead. Write them on your houses and on your gates" (*Dt* 6:4-9). Better yet: I can say to God: Abba! Father; because I am his true son in Jesus Christ. I am, I ought in truth to be, "the image and likeness" of God, who is Love.

———

I shall talk these things over in a colloquy:

• with the Father "from whom every family in heaven and on earth takes its name" (*Ep* 3:15). I shall recall these words from the Epistle to the Romans (12:1): "And now, brothers, I beg you through the mercy of God to offer your bodies as a living sacrifice holy and acceptable to God, your spiritual worship." I shall humbly ask him for this "love of Christ that surpasses all knowledge", so that I "may attain the fullness of God himself" (*Ep* 3:19).

• with Christ our Lord. I shall speak to his heart. Once again I will tell him, "You have loved me, and you have delivered yourself for me." What should I do for Christ in return?

• with Our Lady, our "Mother of Divine Love".

And I shall complete this contemplation with the *Our Father*. In order to say it well, I shall lose myself in this overwhelming current of love within the Trinity, which goes between the Father, Son and Holy Spirit, then diffuses itself within the heart of every man, and finally returns to the Father through Jesus Christ, now resurrected and exalted. Indeed: Our Father!

The prayer that includes all things within itself and that says everything there is to be said:

"Our Father…"

Prayers

The Fathers of the Church and the greatest authors of mystical prayer have taken great pleasure in commenting on the *Our Father*. We should now better understand why.

There is a Carmelite monastery built near the top of the Mount of Olives. The walls of its cloisters are covered with marble plaques on which the words of the *Pater Noster* are engraved in each of the world's principal languages. Now that we have contemplated God's love, does not such a display seem normal and reasonable?

And so it is that at the very peak of our souls, in the very centre of all that we think and do, the *Lord's Prayer* ought to be inscribed in living letters:

Our Father
Who art in heaven,
Hallowed by thy name.
Thy Kingdom come;
Thy will be done
On earth as it is in heaven.
Give us this day our daily bread,
And forgive us our trespasses,
As we forgive those who trespass against us;
And lead us not into temptation,
But deliver us from evil.

If this retreat has helped us simply to recite the *Our Father* with more faith in our understanding and more love in our heart, its purpose has been achieved. We are more the "sons of God".

To Christ our Lord

Soul of Christ, be my sanctification;
Body of Christ, be my salvation;
Blood of Christ's side, fill all my veins;
Water of Christ's side, wash out my stains;
Passion of Christ, my comfort be;
O good Jesus, listen to me.
In thy wounds I fain would to hide;
Never to be parted from thy side.
Guard me should the foe assail me;
Call me when my life shall fail me.
Bid me to come to thee above,
With thy saints to sing thy love,
World without end.
Amen.

This prayer, whose origin was probably Franciscan, goes back at least to the beginning of the fourteenth century, perhaps to the time of John XXII. It was very popular during the lifetime of St Ignatius.

To Our Lady

Hail, Mary, full of grace!
The Lord is with thee;
Blessed art thou among women,
And blessed is the fruit of thy womb, Jesus.
Holy Mary, Mother of God,
Pray for us sinners,
Now and at the hour of our death.
Amen.

Come O Sanctifying Spirit!
(*Veni Sancte Spiritus*)

Come, O Spirit of sanctity, from the glory of heaven
  and send forth the radiance of your light.
Father of all the poor, light and peace of all hearts,
  come with your countless gifts!
Consoler in desolation; refreshment full of loveliness;
  come, dear friend of my soul!
In weariness send repose;
breathe gently the cool refreshing breeze;
  console the desolate who weep alone.
O Light of beatitude, make our hearts ready;
  come, enter into our souls.
Without your grace, man stands alone;
  he cannot be good or sure.
Cleanse what is soiled; heal what is wounded;
  moisten what is arid.
Bend the stubborn will; warm the cold heart;
  guide the wandering footstep!
Holy Spirit, we beg you to give us grace
  through your sevenfold power.
Give us merit for the present,
and one day beatitude when we have finished
  our earthly sojourn.
Amen. Alleluia!

To the Holy Trinity

Glory be to the Father,
And to the Son,
And to the Holy Spirit;
As it was in the beginning,
is now, and ever shall be,
world without end.
Amen.

A sentence composed by St Ignatius that summarises the *Spiritual Exercises*

"*Sic Deo fide quasi rerum successum omnis a te, nihil a Deo penderet. Ita tamen iis omnem operam admove quasi tu nihil Deus solus omnia sit facturus.*"

Here is a translation of this admirable formula for Christian life and action:

"Trust in God as though the entire success of your affairs depended on you and not at all on God, and at the same time give yourself completely to work as if you were not able to do anything yourself and God alone could do everything."

A Retreat for Everyday Life

Fr Paul Dobson

There are moments when we need some 'time out', away from the busyness and the routine of everyday life. We need prime time to be alone, with ourselves and above all with God.

This handbook provides a down-to-earth, practical 24-step retreat. Adapted for personal or group use, it is inspired by the level-headed spirituality of Fr Ronald Knox. Considered reflections on daily life and the call of the Gospel, together with practical suggestions, lead to the peace that a return to Christ surely brings.

PA26   ISBN 978 1 78469 1 196